Original title:
When I Believed

Copyright © 2024 Swan Charm
All rights reserved.

Author: Paulina Pähkel
ISBN HARDBACK: 978-9916-89-862-8
ISBN PAPERBACK: 978-9916-89-863-5
ISBN EBOOK: 978-9916-89-864-2

A Heart Alight with Faith

In shadows deep, a light does glow,
A heart ablaze, in love we sow.
With every breath, our spirits rise,
In faith's embrace, our fears subside.

The path unknown, yet we will tread,
Where angels walk, our hearts are led.
Through trials vast, with strength we stand,
In faith alone, we seek His hand.

Echoes of Eternal Trust

The whispers soft, a promise clear,
In every trial, He draws us near.
With every doubt, His truth remains,
An echo of love that never wanes.

Through storms of life, a guiding star,
In darkness deep, He's never far.
Our hearts attuned to heaven's call,
In trust, we soar, we shall not fall.

The Dawn of Hope Within

Awake, arise, the dawn is here,
With every ray, dissolve the fear.
In hope we find, a love profound,
A gentle promise, safe and sound.

As flowers bloom in morning's light,
Our spirits lift, renewed in sight.
The whispers soft, a sacred hymn,
In hope's embrace, our lives begin.

Whispers of Grace Unseen

In silent moments, grace appears,
A tender balm that soothes our fears.
With open hearts, we hear the call,
In every whisper, we find our all.

The unseen hand that guides our way,
Through darkest nights, into the day.
With grace, we dance in life's refrain,
In every step, we break the chain.

A Solitary Tear

A solitary tear falls, pure and bright,
It speaks of sorrow, yet holds the light.
In moments of silence, it finds release,
With each drop, the heart finds its peace.

Beneath the weight of trials it flows,
A testament to pain that only one knows.
Yet through this sorrow, a strength then appears,
In the depths of grief, hope conquers fears.

A Glimmer of Faith

In shadows deep, a glimmer reveals,
A whisper of truth that the heart feels.
Though storms may rage and doubts start to rise,
Faith holds the promise beyond the skies.

Each flicker of hope ignites the night,
Guiding the weary to morning's light.
With steps unsteady, yet spirits so bold,
A journey unfolds in a story retold.

Embraced by Grace's Gentle Hand

In the quiet hour, grace gently sings,
With warmth it surrounds, as joy softly clings.
No fear in our hearts, no weight of the past,
For love's gentle touch holds our souls steadfast.

Each moment a gift, each breath a prayer,
In the arms of grace, we are cherished and rare.
When burdens are heavy, and paths seem unclear,
Grace whispers softly, 'You have nothing to fear.'

The Voice of the Unseen Shepherd

Through valleys shadowed, where lost souls roam,
The unseen Shepherd calls each heart home.
With love unyielding, His words bring rest,
He gathers the weary, His flock ever blessed.

In whispers of comfort, He guides our way,
Through trials and tears, there's never dismay.
With truth as our anchor, in Him we find peace,
The voice of the Shepherd brings sweet release.

The Light Shines from Within

In the depths of darkness, a light we find,
It flickers and dances, renewing the mind.
Each spark a reminder of love's gentle grace,
A beacon of hope in our sacred space.

Though storms may arise and shadows may fall,
That light shines forever, a guide for us all.
Let it illuminate paths, both old and new,
For the light that we seek always shines through.

The Fire of Hope Burns Brightly

In the depths of night we find,
A flicker, a glow, a spark divine.
With hearts ablaze, we reach for light,
The fire of hope burns ever bright.

Through trials faced and shadows cast,
We hold the flame, steadfast and fast.
It dances high, it shines so clear,
The fire of hope, it conquers fear.

In every soul, a ember glows,
A promise made when darkness grows.
Together we stand, unbent, unbowed,
The fire of hope speaks strong and loud.

As long as breath and life remain,
We kindle joy out of our pain.
With faith aflame, we will ignite,
The fire of hope, our guiding light.

So let it shine, let it endure,
In flames of love, we find the cure.
With every heartbeat, every fight,
The fire of hope burns boldly bright.

The Symphony of Faith and Doubt

In silence deep, the echoes call,
A harmony that binds us all.
With faith and doubt, we weave our way,
A symphony of night and day.

The notes of fear and love entwine,
A melody divine, a sacred sign.
In every heart, the struggle plays,
The symphony of faith we praise.

The gentle whisper, the thunder's roar,
Each sound a story, each chord a door.
With every step, we dance the tune,
A symphony beneath the moon.

Yet doubt must come, a fleeting guest,
In shadows cast, we seek the blessed.
But through it all, the heartbeats sound,
The symphony of hope surrounds.

So let us sing, let voices rise,
In unity, beneath the skies.
For faith and doubt, in love, we tout,
Together we make a beautiful shout.

A Testament of Unseen Love

In the quiet, where shadows blend,
A love that's true, it has no end.
Though eyes may fail to glimpse its grace,
A testament in every space.

Through trials faced and silence cold,
This love, a promise, never sold.
An unseen bond that ties us tight,
A testament through day and night.

In whispered prayers and gentle touch,
In acts of kindness, oh, so much.
Though words may falter, hearts will speak,
A testament of love unique.

In laughter shared and tears we weep,
In sacred vows that we will keep.
Though miles apart, we're close as blood,
A testament flows like a flood.

So cherish this, our silent vow,
In love's embrace, we're here and now.
With every breath, we rise above,
A testament of unseen love.

The Pathway to Endless Grace

Upon the road where shadows lie,
We walk in faith, our spirits high.
Each step we take, a prayer we trace,
The pathway to enduring grace.

Through valleys low and mountains tall,
In every rise, in every fall.
With open hearts, we seek the place,
The pathway leads to endless grace.

In moments of doubt, we find our light,
Within the darkness, shines so bright.
With hands held tight, we embrace the space,
The journey guided by God's grace.

With every burden, every plea,
We grow through love, perpetually.
In every charm, in every face,
We learn to walk the path of grace.

So step with me on this divine road,
For in our hearts, love's seeds are sowed.
Our spirits lift in every phase,
Together we find endless grace.

Gardens Where Faith Blossoms

In gardens where the lilies sway,
Each petal sings a bright bouquet.
Sunlight drapes the gentle ground,
With whispered prayers, our hopes are found.

The soil rich with dreams untold,
In faith's embrace, our hearts unfold.
Each seed a promise, each leaf a grace,
In the garden's warmth, we seek His face.

The blooms arise, a vibrant choir,
Their colors stir a holy fire.
In every fragrant breath, we see,
The beauty of our unity.

Through trials faced, we learn to grow,
In love's own light, our spirits glow.
The jackdaws gather, prayers take flight,
In gardens where we find our light.

The Canvas of Belief's Colors

Upon the canvas of the sky,
Each color tells of prayers that fly.
With strokes of hope and faith so bright,
We paint our souls in sacred light.

The blues of trust, the reds of grace,
In every hue, His love we trace.
With gentle hands, we craft our fate,
In art, we find a bond so great.

The whispers of the winds do call,
In vibrant hues, He hears our all.
A tapestry of hearts entwined,
In colors bold, our faith aligned.

Each shade unveils a story deep,
In moments shared, our spirits leap.
Together we create and weave,
The canvas where we all believe.

Together in the Sacred Dance

In twilight's glow, we take our stand,
With open hearts, we join His hand.
The rhythm swells, our spirits soar,
In sacred steps, we seek Him more.

The circles drawn in soft embrace,
With every turn, we find His grace.
The music swells, our voices rise,
In harmony, our praises fly.

With every leap, our faith ignites,
In joyous spins, we share the light.
Through every trial, we hold on tight,
Together, we are bound in might.

The dance of life, a holy round,
In unity, our hearts are found.
Together we rise on wings of trust,
In sacred dance, we must, we must.

Harmony Born from Reverent Fear

In quiet still, we bow in prayer,
With reverence taught, we show we care.
In fear of loss, we seek the light,
In humble hearts, we find our sight.

The balance struck, a dance of grace,
In reverent awe, we find our place.
The echoes of a sacred call,
In harmony, we rise, we fall.

With hearts entwined, we face the storm,
In shadows cast, His love keeps warm.
Through trials fierce, we learn and grow,
In fear and faith, our spirits glow.

The notes of peace in sacred rhyme,
In humble steps, we dance through time.
Together bound in love so clear,
In harmony, we conquer fear.

Shadows Lifted by Promise

In the night where fears reside,
A light breaks forth, our hearts abide.
With whispered hope, the shadows flee,
In faith we stand, forever free.

Promises spoken, strong and true,
Guiding us as we seek the view.
Every tear and every sigh,
A testament to reaching high.

Through valleys deep, through storms we walk,
In unity, our spirits talk.
With each step, we find the way,
As love illuminates the day.

Mountains tremble, giants fall,
In His strength, we answer the call.
Together bound by sacred grace,
A journey forged in His embrace.

With hearts uplifted, we rejoice,
In every challenge, hear His voice.
Shadows lifted, hope is sewn,
In this promise, we are home.

The Sacred Flame of Conviction

In the quiet of the night,
A flame ignites, burning bright.
It whispers truths we hold so dear,
In its warmth, we feel no fear.

Through trials faced and struggles won,
The sacred flame shines like the sun.
With steady hands, we guard the light,
Guided by faith through darkest night.

In moments of doubt, it stands tall,
A beacon bright, our sacred call.
With every flicker, doubts disperse,
In conviction's arms, we find the verse.

Hearts ablaze with passion's might,
Together we will share the light.
From soul to soul, it spreads the fire,
In unity, we climb higher.

O flame, eternal, never cease,
In every heart, bring forth your peace.
The sacred truth we hold within,
A journey shared, our souls begin.

Veils of Doubt Torn Asunder

In the twilight where shadows play,
Veils of doubt begin to fray.
With trembling hearts, we seek the way,
To truth's embrace, we'll boldly sway.

Every question, every plea,
In sacred silence, set us free.
Torn asunder, fear's disguise,
In faith's embrace, the spirit flies.

Through trials deep and nights forlorn,
New dawns will rise, the heart reborn.
As burdens lift and burdens share,
In community, we find our care.

The whispers of doubt fade away,
Replaced by light that guides the day.
Veils dissolved in love's pure light,
Our eyes unveiled, behold the sight.

With open hearts, we walk as one,
In the light of the eternal sun.
Together bound, our spirits soar,
Veils of doubt cast out, evermore.

The Covenant of a Faithful Heart

In every promise etched in time,
A covenant deep, a sacred rhyme.
With faithful hearts, we pledge to stand,
Together bound by His guiding hand.

Through storms that rage and trials faced,
In love's embrace, we find our place.
A bond unbroken, strong and true,
Each beating heart beats for the few.

Your sorrows shared, my joys embraced,
In this covenant, we're interlaced.
The faithful heart is never lone,
In unity, our love is sown.

From ancient words to tales of old,
The faithful story still unfolds.
We walk in grace, our spirits free,
In the light of love's decree.

Together we will rise and soar,
In His strength, we'll seek the shore.
The covenant of hearts entwined,
In every beat, His love we find.

The Fire of Belief's Ember

In the heart, a flame resides,
A spark of faith, it gently guides.
Through shadows deep, it brightly glows,
A light of hope that never slows.

In trials faced, its warmth remains,
A shelter soft through life's harsh strains.
With whispered prayers on trembling lips,
We gather strength, our spirits lift.

When doubts arise, the fire burns,
In sacred moments, soft it yearns.
A steady hand, a voice of peace,
In belief's ember, we find release.

The flame ignites in every soul,
Uniting hearts to make us whole.
For in the fire, love's truth is shown,
In every breath, His grace is known.

So hold the ember, keep it near,
In darkest nights, cast out the fear.
For faith will lead through storm and strife,
The fire of belief, the breath of life.

Notes from Heaven's Symphony

In the stillness, angels sing,
Their melodies, a sacred ring.
Each note a prayer, each chord a dream,
A harmony of light agleam.

When morning breaks, the echoes flow,
With songs of love, their presence show.
A gentle breeze, a whispered grace,
In music's arms, we find our place.

Their symphony in twilight fades,
In moonlit nights, the heart invades.
A tune of joy, a tale of hope,
In every heart, we learn to cope.

The strings of fate, they gently pluck,
In every life, the sacred luck.
For in each note, a truth runs deep,
From Heaven's heights, our souls to keep.

Thus listen well, when silence speaks,
In notes divine, our spirit seeks.
For in the symphony of grace,
We find our truest, holy place.

The Fragrance of Sacred Truth

In gardens lush, the flowers bloom,
Each petal holds a sweet perfume.
With every scent, a prayer takes flight,
In fragrant whispers, love ignites.

Through sacred woods, the breezes dance,
A fragrant veil, a holy chance.
To find the truth in nature's sigh,
In every scent, the spirit's cry.

Like incense rising to the sky,
Our hearts uplift, we learn to fly.
In every breath, a promise made,
The fragrance pure, we are remade.

In quiet moments, stillness reigns,
The truth unfolds, breaks all the chains.
With open hearts, we seek to find,
The sacred truth, the love divine.

So let the fragrance fill the air,
In every soul's unspoken prayer.
For in its essence, we are whole,
The fragrance of truth, the path to soul.

Within the Silence of the Heart

In silence deep, our spirits meet,
A quiet place where love's complete.
In whispered prayers and gentle sighs,
The heart reveals where truth abides.

With stillness wrapped, we come to know,
The sacred light that starts to glow.
In every pause, His presence calls,
Within the silence, faith enthralls.

Our thoughts may drift like autumn leaves,
Yet in the calm, the heart believes.
With every beat, a truth expressed,
In silence found, our souls are blessed.

So seek the quiet, hold it dear,
For in this space, He'll draw you near.
Through trials faced and joys imparted,
Within the silence, all is started.

Thus linger here, embrace the peace,
In heartfelt stillness, find release.
For in the silence, love's embrace,
Awakes the heart, reveals His grace.

Songs from the Celestial Realm

In heights where angels sing,
The stars bow in their grace.
A chorus of pure light,
Echoes through time and space.

With wings that touch the skies,
And hearts that beat as one,
We find our sacred peace,
Beneath the glowing sun.

The whispered prayers arise,
Like incense in the air.
Each note a soft embrace,
A promise of His care.

In harmony we dwell,
In unity we rise.
A bond that naught can break,
We soar through endless skies.

Let shadows fall away,
Let love's light be our guide.
In songs from realms divine,
In faith, we shall abide.

Covenant of the Living Spirit

In the hush of morning light,
We gather as one soul.
With hearts ablaze in trust,
We embrace the sacred whole.

A covenant declared,
In whispers soft and sweet.
We walk this path of grace,
With every step, we meet.

The spirit flows through us,
A river ever wide.
It binds us in His love,
In Him, we all abide.

With hands joined in the fight,
We face the trials ahead.
Together we shall stand,
On His word, we are fed.

As dawn brings forth the day,
We rise to greet the call.
In this living spirit,
We shall never fall.

Where Souls Dance with Eternity

In twilight's gentle glow,
We lose all sense of time.
The dance of soul and spirit,
In rhythm taste divine.

With every step we take,
In grace, we find our way.
In laughter and in tears,
We weave the night and day.

Infinite our journey,
With love as our refrain.
Two hearts entwined in trust,
Forever seek His name.

In circles wide and free,
We twirl beneath the stars.
Where echoes of our dreams,
Shatter all our scars.

In this sacred embrace,
Eternity unfolds.
For souls that dare to dance,
In love, the truth is told.

Radiance in the Depths of Silence

In silence pure and deep,
The spirit finds its home.
In stillness, we perceive,
The whispers from the dome.

Each heartbeat sings His name,
A prayer without a sound.
In radiant calm we bask,
In love's embrace, we're found.

Through shadows and through light,
Eternal truth does flow.
In depths where silence reigns,
His presence ever grow.

When words can't hold the worth,
Of all that we can feel,
In quietude, we find,
The grace that makes us heal.

With every breath we take,
In silence, we are one.
A testament of hope,
As life has just begun.

The Promise of the Rising Dawn

In the quiet glow of morning light,
Hope awakens, dispelling the night.
Each ray a promise, tender and true,
A deeper faith in the brightening view.

Birdsong whispers of grace to unfold,
Stories of new beginnings retold.
The sky adorned in hues of gold,
Invites our hearts to be brave and bold.

With every sunrise, a chance to renew,
Casting away the shadows we knew.
Let gratitude rise like the sun's embrace,
For in its warmth, we find our place.

Through trials faced in the dark's retreat,
The dawn reminds us, love is sweet.
In each moment of fleeting despair,
The promise of dawn, always there to share.

So we rise with the sun, hand in hand,
United in faith, we make our stand.
With the promise of hope lighting our way,
We cherish each gift of a brand-new day.

The Echo of Ancient Prayers

Whispers of ages long gone by,
Echo through valleys, under the sky.
Each prayer a thread in the sacred weave,
Binding our hearts in what we believe.

Voices of saints, softly they call,
Reminding us we are never too small.
With every word, a flicker of light,
Guiding our spirits through the endless night.

In the stillness, ancient songs rise,
A chorus of faith that never dies.
Each note a testament, each sigh a plea,
Connecting the past to our present decree.

We gather the echoes, their wisdom profound,
In silence we hear the sacred sound.
With open hearts, we walk the way,
Grounded in hope as we choose to pray.

So let the ancient prayers inform our lives,
With love as the seed from which kindness thrives.
In the rhythm of time, we find our flow,
Carrying forward the prayers we know.

In the Garden of Divine Love

Beneath the boughs of the sacred tree,
A garden blooms, wild and free.
Each petal whispers of grace divine,
In love's embrace, our souls align.

Morning dew, like blessings fall,
Refreshing the spirit, answering the call.
The fragrance of kindness fills the air,
In this haven, all burdens share.

Sunlight dances on leaves so bright,
Illuminating paths with holy light.
Every flower, a memory of peace,
In divine love, our worries cease.

We walk the trails where the heart does sing,
In unity found, we gather and cling.
With every heart beat, we draw near,
In the garden, God's love is clear.

So let us sow seeds of compassion and trust,
Beneath the soil, in faith we must.
For in the garden of love divine,
Eternal blooms shall forever shine.

Surrendering to the Eternal Flow

In the river of time, we float and sway,
Trusting the currents to guide our way.
Letting go of the weight we bear,
Surrendering to love in the open air.

With every wave that whispers so sweet,
Carrying us onward, a rhythmic beat.
In stillness we find our true design,
Unraveling threads of the grand divine.

As seasons change, we learn to embrace,
The dance of life in its sacred space.
With hearts wide open, we learn to fly,
Embracing the winds that carry us high.

In surrendering all, we find our peace,
In the flow of the heart, our troubles cease.
For in letting go, we learn to see,
The beauty of life's vast harmony.

So trust in the tide, release your fears,
For the eternal flow dries not with tears.
In each moment surrendered, love will grow,
And in this surrender, our spirits know.

Unfurling Wings of Faith

In the dawn of hope, we rise,
With wings spread wide, we touch the skies.
Every prayer, a whispered light,
Guiding us through the darkest night.

A gentle breeze, the spirit calls,
Through trials high, and through the falls.
In surrender, we find our way,
With faith that leads, come what may.

Each step a journey, a sacred path,
An echo soft of divine wrath.
With open hearts, we seek to know,
A love that endlessly tends to grow.

The sunbeams dance, a glorious sight,
Illuminating dreams in flight.
Through clouds of doubt, we stay unbowed,
In the arms of grace, forever proud.

As we ascend on wings of prayer,
In unity, a sacred share.
Together we soar, no fear in sight,
Embraced by love, bathed in light.

The Spirit's Sublime Dance

In silence deep, the spirit sways,
Infinite rhythms weave our days.
A melody whispers, soft yet strong,
Entwining hearts in a sacred song.

Each step we take, the grace unfolds,
In every breath, a truth retold.
Through shadows cast, we find our way,
As love's pure light guides our stay.

With joy, we twirl in freedom's sphere,
Each moment shared, a prayer sincere.
In every heartbeat, the dance of life,
Transforming chaos into bright.

Lifted higher, we rise and twine,
In the arms of faith, we brightly shine.
The spirit dances, bold and free,
In every soul, a symphony.

Together we sway, as one we sing,
In harmony, our spirits cling.
The dance of love, a ceaseless fire,
In guiding hands, we find desire.

Patterns of the Eternal Song

The universe hums a timeless tune,
In every star, a sacred rune.
With each heartbeat, the rhythm flows,
An endless cycle of highs and lows.

In whispered winds, the tales unfold,
Of ancient truths that never grow old.
We gather near to hear the call,
Embracing the journey, one and all.

Through valleys deep and mountains high,
The song of life will never die.
In every note, divinity waits,
Unlocking the vast, celestial gates.

Together we weave, a tapestry bright,
In unity's glow, a guiding light.
The patterns shift, yet remain true,
In every heart, the sacred view.

As time spins forth, we dance and sing,
In the chorus of love, our spirits cling.
Each voice a thread in the grand design,
Echoing love, both yours and mine.

Heartbeat of the Divine Presence

In the stillness whispers flow,
A heartbeat strong, a gentle glow.
Within each soul, the pulse is felt,
In sacred bonds, our spirits melt.

Awake, arise, in love we stand,
Together linked by unseen hands.
Through trials vast, through pain and strife,
The heartbeat sings, the song of life.

Echoes of grace, a soothing balm,
In every storm, we find our calm.
With open hearts, we gather near,
In the warmth of love, we need not fear.

The pulse of faith, a sacred guide,
In trust and hope, we shall abide.
With every breath, a prayer we send,
In the heartbeat, we find our friend.

Through unseen ties, we come alive,
In unity's light, we shall thrive.
Held close in grace, we rise to see,
The heartbeat of our divinity.

Pilgrim's Song Under Heaven's Gaze

In the silence of the night, I tread,
Steps of faith where angels led.
With every breath, I seek the way,
Under heaven's gaze, I humbly pray.

Mountains high and valleys low,
Whispers of the wind I know.
Each star a guide, each moon a sign,
In every heart, the light divine.

Through trials faced and burdens borne,
In dawn's embrace, I find reborn.
The path is steep, yet love's my guide,
In every shadow, He'll abide.

I travel forth with spirit light,
Through darkest days, to claim the bright.
With every step upon this ground,
A pilgrim's song in faith resounds.

So lead me on, O light of grace,
In every moment, seek Your face.
With hands held high, my heart will sing,
A journey blessed, my offering.

The Note of a Faithful Heart

In the stillness, a melody plays,
Each note a prayer, in soft arrays.
With rhythms woven of love and light,
The faithful heart sings through the night.

In trials met and fears outgrown,
A symphony of grace is sown.
With open arms, I welcome peace,
In every heartbeat, doubts release.

The chorus rises, pure and true,
In every chord, Lord, I find You.
Your whispers wrap me, gentle and kind,
In every moment, Your love I find.

Through storms that rage and shadows cast,
The note of hope forever lasts.
In every tear, in every smile,
Your presence, Lord, goes every mile.

So let the song of faith resound,
In every corner of the ground.
With every breath, Your name I'll sing,
The note of a heart that's worshipping.

The Gentle Hand of the Guiding Light

In twilight hours when shadows blend,
The gentle hand of grace descends.
With tender touch, it dries the tears,
And soothes the soul and calms the fears.

Through every trial that life may send,
A quiet voice, my truest friend.
It leads me forth on paths unknown,
With love that whispers, I am not alone.

In gardens green and valleys wide,
Your guiding light, my faithful guide.
With every dawn, Your truth unfolds,
In every story, love retold.

The stars above, a testament,
To every prayer, to every lament.
Through darkest nights, I see the spark,
Your gentle hand ignites the dark.

So here I stand, in faith renewed,
Embracing love in gratitude.
With every step, I walk in sight,
The gentle hand of guiding light.

Sanctum of the Serene Soul

In sacred silence, I retreat,
To find the place where heartbeats meet.
Within the sanctum, pure and still,
I rest my spirit, seek Your will.

With fragrant prayers like incense rise,
A gentle peace envelops skies.
In still waters, my spirit lays,
Renewed by love in countless ways.

In whispered truths and sacred sighs,
The sanctum calls, my soul complies.
With every breath, I feel Your grace,
In every moment, Your warm embrace.

With eyes closed tight, I see the light,
Guiding my heart through darkest night.
In quietude, I hear the call,
The voice of Love that conquers all.

So here I dwell, O sacred place,
In every heartbeat, feel Your grace.
The sanctum holds my spirit whole,
A refuge found, the serene soul.

Beneath the Wings of Angels

In prayerful whispers, grace descends,
A soft embrace that never ends.
Guiding light in darkest days,
Where love and mercy fill our ways.

Heaven's messengers take their flight,
Offering shelter, pure and bright.
With each heartbeat, faith draws near,
In sacred moments, calm and clear.

The burdens of the world we share,
Entrusted gently to their care.
In silent hope, they carry forth,
In every soul, they find their worth.

Beneath their wings, we find our peace,
In holy stillness, worries cease.
Together bonded, hand in hand,
In divine trust, together we stand.

With every dawn, a new refrain,
A sacred promise still remains.
In whispered prayers, we lift our eyes,
And find our strength beneath the skies.

The Lanterns of Lost Night

When shadows linger, hope may fade,
Yet lanterns glow in darkness laid.
Through trials deep and tempests strong,
A guiding light calls us along.

In gentle flickers, truth aligns,
Illuminating weary minds.
With faith ignited, hearts shall soar,
To find the blessings evermore.

Humble flickers, souls ignite,
In whispered prayers, we seek the light.
Through barren paths and winding ways,
The lanterns shine, our spirits blaze.

In every heart, a flame remains,
A sacred fire that never wanes.
Through darkest nights and endless streams,
We hold the light of cherished dreams.

United in this sacred quest,
We find the warmth, our souls at rest.
With lanterns bright, we share the glow,
And lift each other as we grow.

A Vessel of Quiet Trust

Within the depths of silent prayer,
A vessel waits, our burdens bare.
In tranquil waters, faith resounds,
Where love encircles, grace abounds.

Each gentle sigh, a whispered plea,
In hidden chambers, souls set free.
With hands uplifted, we release,
A tranquil heart finds perfect peace.

The storms of life may test our will,
Yet anchored deeply, we stand still.
In every trial, a lesson learned,
With quiet trust, our spirits turned.

Through seasons change, we navigate,
With faith that flows, no fear, no hate.
In stillness found, we hear the call,
A sacred promise covers all.

Each moment cherished, light bestowed,
In humble gratitude, we're owed.
A vessel shaped by love divine,
In quiet trust, our hearts entwine.

Threads of Celestial Connection

In woven fabric of the night,
Soft threads of stars, a guiding light.
Each pulse of life, a sacred tie,
In cosmic dance, we soar and fly.

Through every heartbeat, love we feel,
The universe, a sacred reel.
With gentle whispers from above,
We weave our stories, threads of love.

In trials faced, we find our way,
In unity, we rise, we sway.
Embracing all with open arms,
Through celestial bonds, we find our charms.

Connected deeply, hearts align,
In shared reflections, pure and fine.
Through every journey, hand in hand,
In threads of light, together we stand.

In faith, we find our truest form,
A tapestry of love is born.
Through life's vast dance, we are embraced,
With threads divine, our path is traced.

Rivers of Mercy Flowing Free

In the embrace of endless skies,
Rivers of mercy gently rise.
Flowing forth like sacred light,
Washing souls in purest sight.

Graceful whispers through the trees,
Carried softly on the breeze.
Every teardrop finds its home,
In the heart where love has grown.

Beneath the stars, the waters gleam,
Life's reflections in a dream.
Flowing freely, all is one,
From the moon and to the sun.

In the stillness, hope is sown,
Where compassion has been shown.
With each wave, the past relents,
In the river, there's repentance.

From the depths, new life will spring,
On the shores, the angels sing.
Embrace the flow, let it be,
For in mercy, we are free.

Tapestry of the Divine Touch

In woven threads, the spirit dwells,
Stories sung, the heart compels.
Patterns rich in love and grace,
Every stitch a warm embrace.

Colors bright as morning light,
Each a truth, a guiding sight.
With gentle hands, the weaver moves,
Crafting dreams that love improves.

In the quiet, truth is spun,
A sacred dance, a journey begun.
Tapestries of faith unfold,
In the warmth, our hearts are told.

From dark to light, we find a way,
In the fabric of the day.
Every life, a thread so fine,
Together in this grand design.

As we gather, we ascend,
In this art, our souls amend.
In unity, our spirits clutch,
Forever held by divine touch.

Echoes of the Silent Prayer

In the stillness of the night,
Whispers of the soul take flight.
Voices soft and hearts laid bare,
All around, the silent prayer.

Candle flames flicker and dance,
In their glow, we find our chance.
Every breath a sacred sigh,
In this moment, spirits fly.

Beneath the stars, we seek the way,
In our hearts, the words will stay.
For in silence, truth we find,
Forging bonds that intertwine.

Prayer transcends the bounds of time,
A melody, a whispered rhyme.
In the quiet, fears take flight,
Echoes shine, a guiding light.

As we gather, hearts unite,
In harmony, we take delight.
These echoes of love will stay,
Forever in our silent prayer.

The Stillness of Sacred Assurance

In the eye of the storm, we find,
A sacred peace that calms the mind.
With every heartbeat, faith is known,
In the stillness, we feel at home.

Wrapped in the arms of quiet grace,
Life unfolds at a gentle pace.
In the shadows, light appears,
Assurances that calm our fears.

Moments cherished, time stands still,
Every breath, a gradual thrill.
In the whispers of the divine,
We discover grace that intertwines.

As day meets night, the cycle flows,
In sacred stillness, love bestows.
With every dawn, new light produced,
In our hearts, the truth is juiced.

The stillness wraps us in its grace,
Holding us in love's embrace.
Here we stand, forever sure,
In divine peace, we are secure.

The Brush of Grace against the Heart

In silent whispers, grace descends,
A gentle touch, where love transcends.
Hearts, once weary, now embrace,
The light that paints with purest grace.

Forgiveness flows like rivers wide,
In every tear, the Savior's guide.
With every stroke, the past forgone,
A canvas new, our lives reborn.

In shadows deep, where hope grows dim,
The brush of grace restores the hymn.
Each line a promise, bold and clear,
That love will conquer all our fear.

With patient hands, the heart is spun,
Creating beauty, peace begun.
In every heartbeat, lessons learned,
With grace, the soul is softly turned.

As light emerges, darkness fades,
In grace, the heart no longer wades.
It dances free, a sacred part,
Embraced forever, grace on heart.

A Journey into the Heart of Trust

Step by step, through mountains steep,
In quiet whispers, secrets keep.
A journey sown with threads of fate,
Trust leads the way, no need to wait.

With every trial, faith will shine,
A guiding star, forever line.
Through stormy skies and shadows cast,
In trust, we find our anchor fast.

Each stumble soft, a lesson told,
The path unfolds, both brave and bold.
With open hearts, we venture forth,
In trust, we embark to find our worth.

Companions cherished, hand in hand,
Together moving, a loyal band.
The heart of trust, a sacred space,
Where love ignites in warm embrace.

So journey on, with spirits high,
In every tear, a joyful sigh.
For trust is light that never dims,
A journey blessed, as hope begins.

The Wellspring of Resilience

Within the depths, where courage grows,
A wellspring flows, and strength bestows.
In trials faced, we rise anew,
With every breath, resilience too.

The heart like iron, forged in fire,
Emerges strong, and lifts us higher.
With every challenge, roots run deep,
In hope we stand, our dreams to keep.

When heavy burdens weigh us down,
Resilience blooms, a vibrant crown.
A testament to all we bear,
With faith, we find the strength to dare.

In unity, we stand as one,
The light that shines when day is done.
Each whispered prayer, a sturdy thread,
In love's embrace, our spirits fed.

So rise, O heart, and face the storm,
In every struggle, joy is born.
For in the depths, where hope resides,
The wellspring flows, and life abides.

Stars of Conviction in the Night

When darkness falls and shadows creep,
The stars awaken, promises keep.
Shining bright with every truth,
In stillness found, the flame of youth.

With steadfast hearts, we gaze above,
Each star a symbol of our love.
Through trials fierce and tempests thrown,
Our conviction stands, never alone.

In nights of doubt, they guide our way,
A radiant light, come what may.
For every star, a story shared,
Of hope and faith, of hearts ensnared.

Let voices rise, a chorus strong,
In unity, we all belong.
The stars of conviction, bold and bright,
Remind us all to stand and fight.

So as we journey, hand in hand,
In every heart, a star will stand.
Through darkest nights, our hearts ignite,
With stars of hope, we find our light.

Heartstrings Tied to Divinity

In quiet moments, prayers rise,
Heartbeats echo, spirit sighs.
Love flows freely, a gentle stream,
Ties of faith, woven in a dream.

In sacred whispers, passions bloom,
Guided by light, dispelling gloom.
Hands reach upward, yearning embrace,
Every heartbeat finds its place.

Through trials faced, the heart stays true,
In darkness, shines a sacred hue.
Endless mercy, a soft refrain,
In every joy, in every pain.

As dawn breaks forth, grace renews,
In every path, a light imbues.
Unified with the eternal soul,
Together, we make the spirit whole.

With every thread, the fabric grows,
In love divine, our journey flows.
Hearts entwined in a sacred dance,
In divinity, we find our chance.

In the Shadow of Divine Truth

In shadows deep, the soul can stand,
Seeking light, a guiding hand.
Whispers echo in the night,
Yearning hearts, drawn to the light.

Truth flows gently, a river wide,
In humble silence, we abide.
Broken vessels, yet we mend,
In divine mercy, love transcends.

Each tear we shed, a seed to grow,
From trials faced, our spirits glow.
In every doubt, a spark ignites,
In shadows dense, the truth unites.

With every step, the path unfolds,
In sacred stories, love retold.
Light pierces through the veils of night,
In every heart, the flame burns bright.

In unity, we stand as one,
Eclipsing fears, we've just begun.
Guided by faith, our spirits soar,
In the shadow, we seek more.

Trusting in the Unfathomable

In the stillness, whispers call,
To trust the unknown, we must fall.
In endless night, a guiding star,
Through unseen paths, we wander far.

The ocean deep, its secrets hide,
Yet faith is strong, our hearts abide.
In every doubt, let courage reign,
A bond of love, our only chain.

In barren lands, hope takes its flight,
Through stormy skies, we seek the light.
Every heartbeat, a prayer so sweet,
In trusting grace, our souls repeat.

With every breath, we find our way,
In moments lost, we choose to stay.
The tapestry of fate unfolds,
In the unknown, our truth beholds.

Together we rise, united and bold,
In sacred trust, our stories told.
Through every trial, love will prevail,
In the unfathomable, we unveil.

The Path of Endless Grace

Upon the path of grace we tread,
With every step, the heart is led.
In still waters, reflections gleam,
A journey born from hope's sweet dream.

With open arms, the spirit flies,
In love's embrace, no more goodbyes.
Each moment cherished, a sacred space,
In every breath, we find our place.

Through valleys low, and mountains high,
Faith lights the way beneath the sky.
A gentle nudge, in darkness near,
In endless grace, we conquer fear.

With every trial, we learn to rise,
In unity, we seek the skies.
The path unfolds, a vibrant hue,
In endless grace, our hearts renew.

In giving thanks for all we receive,
In love's embrace, we truly believe.
Together we walk, hand in hand,
On the path of grace, forever we stand.

A Journey through the Valley of Belief

In shadows deep, the path we tread,
With faith as light, where doubt has fled.
Each step a prayer, a whisper true,
In valleys wide, our spirits renew.

Though storms may rage and skies be gray,
In trust we stand, not led astray.
Through trials fierce, our hearts will soar,
For hope will lead to promise's door.

The echoes call, the silence speaks,
In gentle winds, our spirit seeks.
With every breath, a chance to see,
The grace that flows in you and me.

We walk together, hand in hand,
In sacred bonds, by God's command.
The valley wide, yet love will bind,
In unity, our souls aligned.

So on we journey, brave and bold,
With hearts of fire, our faith unfolds.
Each moment blessed, each lesson learned,
In steadfast love, our candles burn.

Hands Raised in Reverent Wonder

With open hands, we lift our praise,
To skies above, where love displays.
In reverence deep, we bow the knee,
In humble awe, we claim our plea.

The world is bright with blessings vast,
Each heartbeat echoes love that lasts.
In sacred space, our spirits meet,
Where love and grace allow us to greet.

We see the light in every soul,
In unity we find our whole.
With hands held high, we join as one,
In praise of life, beneath the sun.

From mountain peaks to valleys low,
In every breath, His goodness flows.
With hearts aflame, we gather near,
In moments sweet, we cast out fear.

Forever we will sing His song,
In joy and pain, where we belong.
Hands raised in wonder, spirits free,
In love divine, we find our key.

The Beauty of a Faithful Heart

In quiet moments, beauty swells,
A faithful heart, where love compels.
In every trial, a strength revealed,
Through storms of life, our fate is sealed.

The beauty rests in simple grace,
In loving hands, in warm embrace.
With every tear, a lesson learned,
In faith's embrace, our spirits turned.

A gentle soul, with tender light,
Illuminates the darkest night.
In faithful ways, we find our peace,
A beauty deep that will not cease.

With eyes of hope, the world is bright,
In every heart, a sacred light.
Through trials borne, our wounds will heal,
In faithful love, we learn to feel.

So cherish faith, a jewel rare,
In every heartbeat, every prayer.
The beauty of a faithful heart,
An endless gift, a holy art.

Stars of Love in the Darkened Sky

When night descends, the stars awake,
In darkness deep, our hearts they take.
Each sparkling light, a love profound,
In silent skies, His grace is found.

Through every tear, a star ignites,
A beacon bright in sleepless nights.
In shadows cast, we find our way,
With every twinkle, hope's display.

The universe sings a symphony,
Of love and peace, a harmony.
In cosmic dance, our spirits rise,
As light pierces through the darkest skies.

In every heart, a star is born,
In love's embrace, we are reborn.
As we gaze up, our spirits soar,
For in His love, we can explore.

So when the night holds us in thrall,
Remember love, the greatest call.
For stars of love in darkened sky,
Will guide our hearts as years go by.

In the Garden of Devotion

In the stillness, prayers rise high,
Hearts bloom gently, like the sky.
Each petal whispers sweet decree,
In grace we find our unity.

With every step, our souls align,
Amidst the thorns, the love will shine.
In this haven, hope is sown,
A sacred trust, where seeds are grown.

The sun begets the dawn's embrace,
As shadows dance, we find our place.
With every breath, we lift our voice,
In faith we walk, we make the choice.

Through trials wound, we rise anew,
In every storm, the light breaks through.
Together bound, we rise and sing,
In this garden, joy takes wing.

The leaves will rustle, hymns of grace,
In unity, we find our space.
With open hearts, we join the throng,
In the garden, we all belong.

A Pilgrim's Path to Light

A path well worn, the journey calls,
Through valleys low and mountain walls.
With every step, the spirit glows,
In search of truth, the heart bestows.

With every shadow, wisdom speaks,
In silence deep, the spirit seeks.
Beneath the stars, we find our way,
In humble prayer, we learn to stay.

Through tempests wild, our faith is tried,
In every tear, the Lord provides.
The beacon bright, it guides us home,
In trials faced, we never roam.

In fellowship, we share our plight,
Together strong, we seek the light.
With open arms, we lift the meek,
On this path, the truth we seek.

Each breath a step, on sacred ground,
In every heartbeat, love is found.
Through open eyes, we see the grace,
A pilgrim's heart, in every place.

Cloak of Assurance

Wrapped in grace, a cloak divine,
In every struggle, love will shine.
A gentle warmth, our spirits feel,
In quiet trust, the truth will heal.

Through darkest nights, we find the light,
In whispered prayers, we take our flight.
The fabric woven, threads of hope,
In stormy seas, we learn to cope.

With faith as anchor, souls secure,
In every heart, a love that's pure.
With every tear, we weave a strand,
Together strong, we make a stand.

In bonds of kindness, we're entwined,
With grace abundant, peace aligned.
Through trials faced, we'll never part,
In love's embrace, we find the heart.

A cloak of assurance, soft and wide,
In unity, we shall abide.
With every breath, we hold the line,
In faith we walk, our souls align.

Wings of the Spirit's Embrace

Upon the breeze, the spirit flies,
In every whisper, love abides.
With wings outstretched, we rise above,
In every heart, a song of love.

Through trials fierce, we learn to soar,
In every struggle, we find more.
With open arms, the heavens call,
In unity, we'll stand tall.

From ashes rise, the flame ignites,
In darkness deep, we seek the lights.
A gentle touch, the spirit's guide,
In vibrant hues, love cannot hide.

Together bound, our dreams take flight,
In shared devotion, hearts ignite.
With every beat, we lift the soul,
In love's embrace, we are made whole.

In every moment, grace within,
With wings of faith, we rise again.
In harmony, our spirits sing,
In love's embrace, we find our wing.

Anchored in the Divine

In waters deep, we find our way,
Steered by faith, not fear, nor sway.
With every wave, our hearts set free,
Anchored firm, our souls in thee.

The storms may rage, the night grow dim,
Yet in His light, our hopes do swim.
His promise strong, a beacon bright,
Guiding us through the darkest night.

With every prayer, a tether grows,
A sacred bond, as love bestows.
In quiet trust, we stand aligned,
Embracing grace, our souls enshrined.

Together in the sacred fold,
The warmth of faith, a fire untold.
With lifted hearts, we sing and pray,
Anchored in love, come what may.

Each whispered vow, each sacred sign,
We walk in light, forever thine.
In sweet surrender, we become,
Anchored in the Divine, our home.

Bridges Built on the Foundation of Belief

On sturdy beams, our hearts do soar,
Built with love, forevermore.
Each step we take, a bond renewed,
In faith we clasp, in hope pursued.

The gentle hands that guide our way,
Each moment shared, a bright array.
Together strong, we walk as one,
Bridges rise beneath the sun.

With every word, a spark ignites,
Illuminating darkest nights.
A tapestry of trust we weave,
In the light of grace, we believe.

Through trials faced, our spirits blend,
In unity, we shall transcend.
With hearts ablaze, we find our peace,
In bridges strong, our souls release.

For love unites, and faith entwines,
With every step, a path refines.
In truth we stand, no fear, no grief,
Bridges built on the foundation of belief.

Threads of Light in a Frayed World

In shadows deep, where hope seems lost,
We weave our dreams, not counting cost.
With every thread, a story spun,
Threads of light, our race begun.

Each fragile strand, a testament,
To love that binds, to souls content.
In gentle hands, we shape our fate,
As light breaks through, we hesitate.

Though frayed and worn, the path we tread,
In faith we walk, where angels led.
Each tiny spark ignites the night,
We stand as one, transformed by light.

In whispered prayers, our wishes rise,
A symphony that never dies.
With courage kind and hearts so bold,
Threads of light in a frayed world hold.

Together bound by grace divine,
We thread our lives, as stars align.
Emerging bright, our spirits gleam,
In unity, we weave the dream.

The Tides of Trust

In the stillness of the night,
Faith whispers like the sea.
Waves of hope wash over me,
Anchored in love's embrace.

Through storms that shake the shore,
I hold steadfast to the light.
With every rise and fall,
My heart learns to believe.

In trials, I find my strength,
Each tear a lesson learned.
Trust blossoms like the dawn,
Spreading warmth in my soul.

The tides may shift and churn,
Yet I remain secure.
In the heart of chaos,
A peace that ever stays.

Together, we shall sail,
Through the currents of despair.
Guided by a loving hand,
To shores of endless grace.

The Open Door of Understanding

In shadows where doubts linger,
A door stands wide and true.
With each step towards wisdom,
New light begins to break.

Compassion opens vistas,
Where hearts can truly meet.
In the silence of listening,
Understanding takes its form.

Through the veil of prejudice,
I traverse with gentle care.
With love as my compass,
Every soul becomes a guide.

Each question brings a blessing,
In the search for common ground.
Together we build bridges,
Over rivers of our minds.

Embrace the warmth of trust,
Let barriers fall away.
With open hearts and doors,
We journey to the light.

Sanctuary Found in Spiritual Surrender

In the quiet of the heart,
I find my sacred space.
Surrender to the moment,
Opens pathways to grace.

Letting go of the burden,
Dissolving all my fears.
In the arms of mercy,
The soul finds refuge near.

Amidst the clamor of life,
Whispers of peace arise.
In surrender, strength is found,
Faith's anchor holds me tight.

Each breath a prayer of trust,
In stillness, I am whole.
The sanctuary of spirit,
Fosters love in my soul.

With humble hearts we gather,
In unity we stand.
In spiritual surrender,
We open to His hand.

The Radiance of Trusting Eyes

In eyes that shine with hope,
A world begins to glow.
With every glance of kindness,
Trust begins to grow.

In moments of connection,
Souls intertwine and blend.
Reflecting the divine light,
In every heart, a friend.

Through trials, our gaze remains,
Fixed on the path ahead.
In trusting eyes, we see,
The love that gently leads.

With faith, we confront our doubts,
Each challenge met with grace.
In the radiance of trust,
A beauty none can erase.

Together, let us wander,
In this journey of the heart.
With trusting eyes, we witness,
The sacredness of art.

Oaths Whispered to the Divine

In the stillness of the night, we pray,
Hearts entwined in sacred dance,
Voices lifted, fears kept at bay,
With faith we seek our second chance.

Every whisper, a solemn vow,
To guide us through the tempest's roar,
In seeking truth, we humbly bow,
Our spirits yearn for something more.

Beneath the stars, our dreams take flight,
Anointed by the morning dew,
In the quiet, find the light,
A bond renewed, forever true.

The echoes of our souls align,
With blessings flowing from above,
In sacred moments, hearts combine,
A tapestry of grace and love.

So hand in hand, we tread this way,
Guided by a love divine,
In every prayer, we find our sway,
Oaths whispered, a lifeline's sign.

The Fortress of Steadfast Belief

In the heart of shadows, we stand tall,
A fortress built on faith alone,
Through trials fierce, we never fall,
With every prayer, our courage grown.

Walls of hope, unyielding grace,
Lifting spirits, casting fears,
Within this sacred, holy space,
We find the strength to dry our tears.

Around us storms may meet and clash,
Yet anchored firm, our hearts remain,
Through thunder loud, through silence rash,
Our steadfast love, a sweet refrain.

In unity, we share our dreams,
Forge bonds that time can never break,
With each belief, a new light beams,
Together we rise, for love's own sake.

This fortress stands, a beacon bright,
In darkness deep, we touch the dawn,
Through every challenge, we ignite,
The flame of love that carries on.

Illuminated by the Light of Hope

In the valley of despair, we tread,
Seeking rays of dawn anew,
With hearts ablaze, we forge ahead,
Through whispered prayers, we are renewed.

The light descends upon our face,
A gentle warmth that calms our fears,
In shadows deep, we find our place,
With every beam, our vision clears.

Hope is a lantern, bright and bold,
Guiding us through the longest night,
In every tear, a story told,
In every smile, a glimpse of light.

Together walking, side by side,
We share the burdens, share the grace,
With every step, we turn the tide,
In unity, we find our space.

Illuminated, hearts entwined,
A symphony of faith and trust,
In love's embrace, our souls aligned,
Forever cherished, pure and just.

In the Embrace of Endless Grace

In the warmth of your embrace,
We find the solace that we seek,
With every breath, we know our place,
In the quiet, love's whispers speak.

Generous heart, you hold us near,
Through every storm, you calm the sea,
In your grace, we shed our fear,
Together, we are truly free.

Moments fleeting, yet divine,
In every touch, a piece of you,
Our spirits dance, as stars align,
With every prayer, we are renewed.

In the tapestry of night and day,
Each thread a bond, each hue a truth,
We journey forth, come what may,
In endless grace, we find our youth.

So let us walk, hand in hand,
Through valleys deep, on mountains high,
In the embrace, we understand,
With love immortal, we touch the sky.

The Altar of Unwavering Trust

At the altar, hearts lay bare,
In the silence, whispered prayer.
Faith ignites the flickering flame,
In His presence, we are the same.

With each promise, fear does cease,
In His arms, we find our peace.
Even shadows fade away,
Guided by His light, we pray.

Hands uplifted, spirits soar,
In surrender, we seek more.
Every doubt begins to flee,
Bound in love, we're truly free.

Through trials faced, we hold fast,
In our hearts, His love is cast.
With unwavering faith, we stand,
In the warmth of His gentle hand.

Together we will walk this road,
Empowered by the love bestowed.
At the altar, truth we find,
In the Divine, our hearts aligned.

Reflections on the Sacred Waters

By the waters, calm and clear,
Whispers echo, hearts draw near.
In the depths, our souls take flight,
Sinking sorrows, rising light.

Gentle ripples soothe the mind,
In this place, hope we find.
Mirrored skies and tranquil dreams,
Flowing grace in silver streams.

Each reflection tells a tale,
Of the love that will not fail.
As the currents braid our past,
In His mercy, we are cast.

In the sacred, voices blend,
Nature's hymn, our spirits mend.
Every droplet, every sigh,
Carries prayers up to the sky.

Here we gather, hearts entwined,
In the waters, peace defined.
May our faith, like rivers, run,
United under moon and sun.

Beyond the Veil of Doubt

In the stillness, shadows wane,
Breaking through the veil of pain.
Hope emerges in the night,
Guided by eternal light.

Every question finds its grace,
In the silence, we embrace.
Boundless love dispels the fear,
Whispers of the Lord draw near.

Hearts once heavy, now set free,
In His hands, we learn to see.
Through the trials, we ascend,
Faith, the means to reach the end.

Cloaked in doubt, we rise anew,
Every moment, fresh and true.
Beyond the darkness, faith ignites,
In the heart, His love unites.

With each step, the path unfolds,
In surrender, courage molds.
Beyond the veil, our spirits sing,
In His grace, forever cling.

Gathering Clouds of Promise

In the heavens, clouds convene,
Promises made, yet unseen.
Each shadow brings a gentle rain,
That nourishes the world's domain.

Through the storms, our faith will rise,
With His guidance, we'll be wise.
Every drop a sacred gift,
Filling hearts and causing lift.

Beneath dark skies, the light shall break,
Hope ignites for love's own sake.
Gathering storms, a harbinger,
Of the blessings that will stir.

In the distance, thunder rolls,
Awakening our weary souls.
With each rumble, we stand bold,
Trusting in the story told.

Gathering clouds line the way,
In our hearts, we choose to stay.
Beneath the weight, His love will show,
In every promise, we will grow.

Echoes of Faith's Embrace

In shadows deep, where silence plays,
The heart finds peace in prayerful ways.
Each whispered word, a gentle plea,
God's love surrounds, embraces me.

Upon the hill where angels tread,
I cast my doubts and fears, their thread.
With faith as strong as mountains high,
I soar above, my spirit nigh.

The river flows, a sacred song,
In every drop, I feel I belong.
With open arms, the heavens call,
In faith's embrace, I will not fall.

The stars above, they gleam with grace,
Reflecting love in every space.
I walk this path, my heart ablaze,
In Echoes of faith, my soul stays.

In twilight's glow, my worries cease,
I find my solace, I find my peace.
The courage near, I will not shake,
In every step, my soul awake.

Whispers in the Sacred Vale

In valleys low, where spirits dwell,
The whispering winds begin to tell.
Of ancient truths and stories bright,
In the sacred vale, I seek the light.

Each rustling leaf, a prayer on air,
With every breath, I find despair.
Yet hope resounds in every heart,
In nature's hymn, we play our part.

The mountain stands, a witness proud,
To every tear and every crowd.
In silence clad, the world may cease,
But in the vale, I find my peace.

The flowers bloom with colors bold,
A canvas rich in stories told.
In every petal, love's refrain,
Whispers of faith dance like the rain.

And as I walk the paths of grace,
I see the light in every face.
Together we rise, no soul to fail,
In the echoes of the sacred vale.

The Morning Star of Hope

Awakening dawn, the sky ablaze,
With rays of warmth, the night decays.
In every hue, a promise gleams,
The Morning Star ignites our dreams.

Each heart rejoices, a song anew,
The world transformed in golden hue.
With every breath, we rise to greet,
The light of hope, so pure and sweet.

The shadows flee, the dark retreats,
In every soul, the passion beats.
Together we stand, hands entwined,
In unity, our hearts aligned.

The path ahead is bright and clear,
With faith as guide, we have no fear.
For in this moment, grace abounds,
In the Morning Star, our joy resounds.

With eyes uplifted, spirits soar,
We dance in light forevermore.
Each hopeful spark, a brilliant flame,
The Morning Star calls out our name.

Dreams of the Unseen Light

In the realm where shadows play,
The unseen light draws night to day.
With every hope and every prayer,
I chase the dreams, the faith laid bare.

Each heart is filled with silent yearn,
For wisdom gained, and lessons learned.
Through trials faced and burdens shared,
In unseen light, our spirits bared.

The canvas broad, my thoughts take flight,
Imbued with love, the purest sight.
In every dream, God's whispers guide,
Through valleys low, we walk with pride.

The lantern bright, it shines within,
Illuminates where once was sin.
With every step, I learn to trust,
In dreams of light, my soul is thrust.

And when the night creeps close and tight,
I hold the glow of unseen light.
For every dark, there shines a way,
In dreams of faith, I choose to stay.

The Embrace of the Eternal

In shadows deep, His light does dwell,
A soft embrace, where hearts can swell.
Guided by grace, we find our way,
In wisdom's arms, we choose to stay.

With every breath, a sacred song,
In silence' peace, we all belong.
He whispers love, a gentle call,
In the embrace, we never fall.

The stars align, His love adorned,
In unity, our spirits warmed.
Through trials faced, we rise in trust,
In the embrace of the Eternal, we must.

The winds of fate, they bend and sway,
Yet in His arms, we find our way.
The bond of faith, a tether strong,
In every heartbeat, we belong.

So lift your heart to skies above,
In joy and peace, we bask in love.
Together we walk, hand in hand,
In the embrace, forever we stand.

Reverie of the Sacred Path

Upon the road, the sacred light,
Illuminates the darkest night.
In every step, a promise true,
The path unfolds, and we renew.

With open hearts, we heed the call,
As love descends, we rise and fall.
The sacred echo, soft and clear,
Guides weary souls, dispels all fear.

In nature's hush, we find Him there,
A whisper shared upon the air.
In every breeze, His presence near,
A gentle nudge, forever dear.

The journey winds through trials bold,
Each moment rich, each story told.
With every dawn, we breathe anew,
On sacred paths, we find the true.

So let us walk, both brave and free,
In reverie, our spirits see.
A love that binds, a truth profound,
On sacred paths, our hearts unbound.

The Horizon of Belief Reaches Beyond

At dawn's first light, the heavens greet,
A horizon wide, where dreams compete.
In belief, we rise, we soar on high,
As faith ignites our spirits nigh.

The whispers of hope, like waves on shore,
Remind us all that we are more.
With every trial, a lesson learned,
In our hearts, the flame has burned.

Beyond the stars, our burdens cast,
In love's embrace, we're free at last.
For every tear that waters the ground,
A blossom blooms, in grace profound.

Through valleys low and mountains steep,
Our beliefs a promise we shall keep.
The horizon stretches, vast and wide,
In unity, we walk with pride.

So let us reach, our hands held high,
With hearts ablaze beneath the sky.
In faith we stand, together strong,
The horizon beckons, where we belong.

Serenity Found in Quiet Trust

In silence deep, the spirit breathes,
Through gentle sighs, the heart believes.
In quiet trust, we lay our fears,
With every prayer, the soul appears.

The stillness wraps, a tender shroud,
In sacred peace, we stand unbowed.
In moments soft, the blessings flow,
Serenity's grace, we come to know.

A whisper sweet, the world grows still,
In faith's embrace, we seek His will.
With open arms, we hold the light,
And walk in love, dispelling night.

When storms arise, and doubts invade,
In quiet trust, our fears will fade.
For in the depth of faith's firm grace,
We find our home, our sacred space.

So breathe in calm, let worries cease,
In serenity, we find our peace.
Together, strong, we rise above,
In quiet trust, we walk in love.

The Pilgrim's Heart Awakened

In shadows cast by doubt and fear,
A traveler seeks a path made clear.
With faith as guide and hope to steer,
The heart awakens, drawing near.

Each step a prayer, each breath a song,
Embracing grace where they belong.
The lessons learned, both brave and strong,
In a world where souls weave along.

Mountains rise, though storms may rage,
Yet joy unfolds on every page.
With reverence, they turn the age,
In unity, they set the stage.

The lantern's glow, a gentle spark,
Illuminates the pathway dark.
In whispers soft, the spirits hark,
As love ignites within the heart.

Through trials faced, a truth revealed,
In open arms, the wounds are healed.
The pilgrim's badge, a fate sealed,
In sacred light, their fate concealed.

A Tapestry Woven with Light

Threads of mercy, woven tight,
In vibrant hues, dispelling night.
Each strand a story, pure delight,
Together form a tapestry bright.

In gentle hands, the loom does smile,
Creating grace, a soul's true trial.
With every knot, a sacred mile,
And unity becomes the style.

Colors blend from hearts sincere,
In harmony, they draw us near.
With every thread, the hope is clear,
A grand design, divinely sheer.

Upon this cloth, our dreams unroll,
A symphony that soothes the soul.
Each woven piece, a precious goal,
In love's embrace, we become whole.

Our spirits dance, entwined in grace,
Within this fragrant, sacred space.
A tapestry, the truth we chase,
In every heart, a holy trace.

Serene Valleys of Belief

In valleys deep, where silence dwells,
The spirit sings of ancient spells.
Here faith resides, and magic swells,
In whispers soft, the heart compels.

The river flows through sacred ground,
In every ripple, truth is found.
With open arms, we gather 'round,
In peace and love, our souls unbound.

Among the trees, a sheltering shade,
Where every tear of joy is laid.
In gratitude, our fears do fade,
As nature's hymn serenely played.

The mountains stand, a royal throne,
Where echoes roam, and dreams are grown.
In these valleys, love has shown,
An everlasting faith we've sown.

With every breeze, a tender kiss,
In harmony, we find our bliss.
In gentle hands, the world we miss,
And in this peace, our hearts persist.

The Language of Sacred Stillness

In sacred calm, where echoes cease,
A quiet song brings heart to peace.
In every pause, a sweet release,
The language whispered, soft as fleece.

When silence speaks, the soul can hear,
The hidden truths that draw us near.
In every breath, a promise clear,
A call to hold the moment dear.

With gentle light, the spirit glows,
In stillness deep, the current flows.
A world of wonder, love bestows,
Where every thought of kindness grows.

Across the landscape, soft and wide,
In tranquil waters, hearts abide.
With every pulse, we turn the tide,
In sacred stillness, love will guide.

Through ancient paths, where shadows tread,
In quiet grace, our fears are shed.
In harmony, our spirits fed,
In sacred stillness, hope is bred.

Seeds of Faith Sown in Trials

In the garden of our woes, we stand,
Planting seeds with trembling hand.
Through storms and shadows, faith will grow,
In every trial, His love we sow.

The roots dig deep in sorrow's ground,
With every tear, a promise found.
When hope seems lost, look to the skies,
For in the dark, true faith will rise.

Tended by grace, the blossoms appear,
A testament to love held dear.
Each trial faced, a chapter told,
In the book of faith, a story bold.

So let us walk, though pain may bite,
With hearts aflame, igniting light.
For in the struggle, strength is born,
Our faith, like morning, sweetly worn.

In every heartache, seeds we'll sow,
Cultivating what He calls us to know.
With faith as our guide, we forge ahead,
In every trial, His love is spread.

The Song of the Undying Spirit

Awake, O heart, the dawn is near,
In shadows deep, let go your fear.
For every wound shall speak of grace,
The song of life, our sacred place.

Through valleys low and mountains high,
The spirit sings, it cannot die.
With every breath, a note of praise,
A melody that never sways.

In quiet moments, truth will rise,
As whispers dance in evening skies.
Each trial faced, each burden borne,
A symphony of hope is born.

The chorus swells with every tear,
In joy and pain, our song draws near.
With faith as our foundation stone,
In harmony, we're never alone.

So sing, dear soul, through night and day,
Let love's sweet music light the way.
For in the darkest, deepest night,
The song of spirit shines so bright.

Paths Paved by Sacred Promises

In every step, a promise found,
As faith leads forth, on hallowed ground.
With every dawn, His word shines bright,
Guiding us through the darkest night.

The road is long, with twists and turns,
Yet in our hearts, His promise burns.
Through trials faced, His light will gleam,
Illuminating every dream.

With hands held high, we seek His face,
In every season, feel His grace.
For every path we boldly tread,
Is paved with love, where angels led.

So let us walk with hearts renewed,
Wherever He leads, we'll be imbued.
In every moment, trust shall reign,
For sacred promises break every chain.

In faith, we find the strength to rise,
For in His arms, all darkness dies.
Through valleys low and mountains steep,
We'll follow Him, our souls to keep.

A Grain of Faith in the Tempest

Amidst the storm, a whisper calls,
In raging seas, His promise falls.
A grain of faith, a beacon bright,
To guide us through the longest night.

The winds may howl, the waters clash,
Yet in His arms, the fears all dash.
With every wave that threatens sway,
His love will anchor, come what may.

In trials fierce, where shadows creep,
His presence near, a comfort deep.
So cast your cares upon His shore,
For faith will rise, forevermore.

When tempests roar and doubts unfold,
Hold fast, dear heart, to what He told.
For in the storm, He walks with grace,
A steadfast love, our refuge place.

So let us trust, though legions fight,
In faith's embrace, we find our light.
Through every tempest, we'll proclaim,
With grains of faith, we call His name.

The Bridge Between Earth and Sky

In stillness, the whispers sing,
Of heavens wide and earth's embrace,
Between the realms, the angels bring,
A harmony of boundless grace.

Where sunlight meets the morning dew,
The bridge connects, a sacred thread,
Each step adorned in love so true,
A path where hope and faith are fed.

Clouds part to reveal skies so bright,
A canvas painted with divine,
The heart ignites, a beacon's light,
As spirits dance in pure design.

In nature's breath, we find our way,
The pulse of life, both bold and mild,
With every heartbeat, night and day,
We walk as pilgrims, free and wild.

So lift your eyes, O wayward soul,
Embrace the call of heaven's choir,
For in the harmony, we're whole,
United where the heart's desire.

Illuminated by Grace's Touch

A shadow lifts, the dawn appears,
With grace, it drapes the world in light,
Each moment quenches hidden fears,
A promise shines, so warm, so bright.

From every tear, a jewel forms,
Reflecting hope, a sacred gift,
In trials faced, the spirit warms,
Through grace, the soul begins to lift.

The gentle breeze, a whispered prayer,
Carries our burdens through the night,
In every heartbeat, love laid bare,
A touch divine, profound and right.

Together we rise, hands held high,
Across the valleys, fields, and streams,
With every step, we touch the sky,
Unfolding life's eternal dreams.

May grace surround, like morning dew,
Illuminating paths uncharted,
In unity, our spirits grew,
Awakened souls, once broken-hearted.

Embracing the Divine within

In silence, the sacred whispers call,
A journey inward, deep and wide,
Embracing grace, we rise and fall,
Within the heart, the truth resides.

With every breath, the spirit wakes,
A vibrant dance, a fiery glow,
In love's embrace, a path it makes,
To forge a bond with depths we know.

The mirror shows the light we bear,
Reflecting strength in gentle ways,
Through trials faced, our hearts laid bare,
Revealing love's unending praise.

Let go of fear, the shadows flee,
For in the depths, the soul expands,
In unity, we become free,
Connected through the heart's own hands.

So walk this path with open eyes,
Embrace the divine, the light within,
In every heartbeat, love replies,
Finding the strength to begin again.

A Journey through the Fields of Hope

Across the fields where wildflowers bloom,
A journey begins with sky's embrace,
Where dreams like stars dispel the gloom,
In heart's deep soil, we find our place.

Each step we take is laced with prayer,
A tapestry of faith and love,
Through seasons' change, with courage rare,
We venture forth, guided from above.

The rivers flow with wisdom's song,
Carrying whispers of ancient days,
In unity, we all belong,
With open hearts, in light we blaze.

Through trials faced, we find our strength,
Resilient as the bending trees,
In every moment, love's great length,
A nurturing force felt in the breeze.

So tread these fields, O weary soul,
With hope as your unfailing guide,
In every step, let healing roll,
For in each heart, true love resides.

Lanterns in the Night of the Soul

In darkness deep, the lanterns shine,
Guiding hearts through trials divine.
Whispers of hope in shadows cast,
Illuminating paths to peace at last.

Each flicker tells of love embraced,
A testament of grace interlaced.
In every flicker, a prayer's flight,
Lanterns flicker in the night.

In the quiet, their glow reveals,
The secrets that the spirit feels.
With every breath, we'll find the way,
Lanterns shining till break of day.

Through storms that rage and tempests roar,
These beacons call to souls implore.
Together we rise, hearts intertwined,
In unity, true love defined.

So carry forth this sacred light,
A flame of faith to guide our flight.
With every step, let kindness bloom,
Lanterns in the night dispel all gloom.

Harmony in the Quiet Chorus

In stillness found, a chorus sings,
Voices blend, the heart takes wing.
Each note a whisper of divine grace,
In harmony, we find our place.

The gentle breeze carries our prayer,
Melodies woven with love and care.
Each soul enjoined in sacred dance,
In quiet moments, hearts advance.

Together we rise, a symphony,
Echoing hopes through eternity.
With each refrain, spirits align,
In the quiet, a love divine.

Through trials faced and burdens borne,
The chorus swells, our hearts are worn.
Yet in this song, we find our strength,
In every verse, we go the length.

So let us sing, with voices bright,
A harmony that brings forth light.
In unity, our souls compose,
A quiet chorus that ever grows.

The Bridge of Unwavering Trust

Spanning the chasm of doubt and fear,
A bridge of trust, steadfast and clear.
With every heartbeat, we cross as one,
Unyielding path, till our journey's done.

Hand in hand, we tread the way,
In faith we rise, come what may.
Each step is guided by love's embrace,
The bridge of trust, a sacred space.

Through shadows cast by life's design,
We walk this path, your hand in mine.
With whispered prayers and voices raised,
United we stand, together praised.

In every stumble, we find our grace,
The bridge withstands, our hearts embrace.
In moments of doubt, our spirits soar,
Faithful and true, we shall endure.

So let us cross this bridge today,
With open hearts, come what may.
Together we'll find the strength we need,
On this unwavering path, we lead.

Cradle of Serene Confession

In whispered tones, our truths unfold,
A cradle of peace, where hearts are bold.
Each confession softens the sting,
In love's embrace, we find our wings.

With every word, the spirit sings,
Releasing burdens, the joy it brings.
A safe haven for weary souls,
In this sacred space, healing rolls.

The night may darken, fears may creep,
Yet in this cradle, secrets keep.
With gentle hands, we hold each tear,
In faith and trust, we persevere.

Together we seek the light above,
In the cradle, we find our love.
Each confession lights the way,
As we journey toward a brighter day.

So come, dear friend, lay down your pain,
In this cradle, hope's refrain.
With open hearts, we rise as one,
In serene confession, our spirits run.

The Weaver's Hands of Destiny

In shadows deep where silence dwells,
The weaver crafts with sacred spells.
Threads of fate in colors bright,
Entwined in dreams, embrace the light.

Each knot a prayer, each twist a song,
Guiding souls where they belong.
With every pull, a path is spun,
In the tapestry, we are one.

From moments lost, to futures found,
The weaver's wisdom knows no bound.
In every heart, a pattern flows,
The hands of love, the heart well knows.

Through trials met and battles fought,
The weaver's hands hold all we've sought.
In sacred trust, we weave our fate,
In the loom of time, we celebrate.

So let us join, let threads entwine,
As we embrace the grand design.
For in the weave, a truth we see,
Our lives are woven, you and me.

A Testament of Unseen Forces

In the quiet hum of the night,
The stars align with divine light.
Whispers float on the gentle breeze,
A testament written in trees.

Invisible hands guide our way,
Through trials faced, through fears we lay.
In every heartbeat, a rhythm flows,
Unseen forces that nobody knows.

With grace, they touch each living soul,
Binding us all, making us whole.
In shadows cast by the moon's embrace,
Guiding our steps, a sacred trace.

We dance through storms, we walk through fire,
Embracing dreams, igniting desire.
For in the silence, their voice is clear,
A testament we hold dear.

So let us trust in the unseen grace,
In the gentle pull, we find our place.
For every moment that we share,
Is woven with love, beyond despair.

Divine Whispers in the Wilderness

In the wilderness where shadows creep,
Divine whispers call, secrets to keep.
Among the trees, in the rustling leaves,
The heart of nature gently believes.

Echoes of faith in the mountain's sigh,
Remind us of love, as time drifts by.
The rivers flow with a sacred song,
In this wild space, we all belong.

Beneath the stars, a promise lies,
As galaxies twinkle in starlit skies.
Each step we take, in love's embrace,
A sacred journey, a holy place.

The winds carry prayers we cannot speak,
In silence found, we seek the meek.
Nature's heart holds a gentle guide,
In wilderness vast, the truth abides.

So let us wander, let us roam,
In divine whispers, we find our home.
For in the wild, where spirits soar,
We meet the love, forever more.

The Embrace of Everlasting Light

In twilight's glow, the shadows yield,
To the embrace of light, our hearts are healed.
A golden touch upon weary eyes,
In the sacred warmth, our spirit flies.

With every dawn, a promise clear,
The eternal light draws ever near.
It dances gently on the soul's face,
A beacon of love, a boundless grace.

Through valleys low and mountains high,
We journey forth, beneath the sky.
In trials faced, in love's delight,
We find our way to everlasting light.

In every heartbeat, we discover peace,
The light within that will not cease.
For in the darkness, it softly gleams,
Guiding our paths, fulfilling dreams.

So let us bask in this holy flame,
In the embrace of light, we are not the same.
For through this love, our souls take flight,
In the embrace of everlasting light.